Preparing a
Budget

Pocket Mentor Series

The *Pocket Mentor* Series offers immediate solutions to common challenges managers face on the job every day. Each book in the series is packed with handy tools, self-tests, and real-life examples to help you identify your strengths and weaknesses and hone critical skills. Whether you're at your desk, in a meeting, or on the road, these portable guides enable you to tackle the daily demands of your work with greater speed, savvy, and effectiveness.

Books in the series:

Preparing a Budget

Expert Solutions to Everyday Challenges

Harvard Business Press

Boston, Massachusetts

ISBN: 978-1-4221-2884-8

The paper used in this publication meets the requirements of the American National
Standard for Permanence of Paper for Publications and Documents in Libraries and
Archives Z39.48-1992.

Contents

Categorizing Expenses   23

How to define various costs in your budget.

Preparing an Operating Budget   33

Eight steps you need to take.

Preparing a Capital Budget   51

A closer look at this type of budget.

When Your Budget and Reality Differ 57

Suggestions for understanding and responding to variance.

What is variance?   58

What causes it?   59

Tips and Tools   61

Tools for Preparing a Budget   63

Worksheets to help you prepare and track an annual budget, ensure that you're covering all the basics in your budget, and create a cash budget for the fiscal year.

Test Yourself   69

A helpful review of concepts presented in this guide. Take it before and after you've read the guide, to see how much you've learned.

Answers to test questions   72

Key Terms   75

To Learn More   79

Further titles of articles and books if you want to go more deeply into the topic.

Sources for Preparing a Budget   85

Mentor's Message: The Power of a Well-Prepared Budget

It's budget time again. And if you're a new manager, you may find the process of preparing a budget a bit intimidating. After all, there's more than one type of budget and more than one way to approach the budgeting process. You'll need to be sure that the budget you prepare will reflect an action plan that's right for your department and company. A thoughtfully prepared budget is a powerful tool for any enterprise, as it helps companies evaluate managers' effectiveness and lay out plans for achieving important strategic goals.

This book walks you through the process of preparing a budget. We'll explore the benefits of budgeting, examine the various types of budgets and approaches to budgeting, and explore ways to categorize expenses—a key element in preparing a budget. Then you'll discover practical steps for preparing an operating budget and a capital budget and for deciding how to respond if your department's actual business results don't match what was reflected in your budget.

Knowing how to prepare a budget is a key responsibility for any manager. This book helps you master the process.

V. G. Narayanan, Mentor

V. G. Narayanan teaches both basic and advanced courses in financial and accounting topics to MBA and doctoral students at Harvard Business School, where he is the Thomas D. Casserly Jr. Professor of Business Administration. He believes that budgets must accomplish more than control purposes to serve an organization well. He consults with numerous businesses and has a special interest in managerial accounting. V. G. has contributed articles to accounting journals and has published many case notes for the school. He is a graduate of Stanford University, where he received his MS in statistics, MA in economics, and PhD in business. His ability to make difficult concepts comprehensible is evidenced in this topic on budgeting, which has a practical approach.

Preparing a Budget: The Basics

An Overview
of Budgeting

A S A MANAGER, you may be asked to prepare a budget for your department or business unit. But what is a budget, exactly? How does budgeting work, and why is preparing a well-thought-out budget important? Let's take a closer look at these questions below.

What is a budget?

A *budget* is the financial blueprint or action plan for a department or organization. It translates strategic plans into measurable expenditures and anticipated returns over a certain period of time.

Budgeting activities include:

- Forecasting future business results, such as sales volume, revenues, capital investments, and expenses

- Reconciling those forecasts to organizational goals and financial constraints

- Obtaining organizational support for your proposed budget

- Managing subsequent business activities to achieve budgeted results

If you have profit and loss responsibility, the difference between the financial results of your division or business unit and the budget may be a key factor in evaluating your job perform-ance. This difference may also be tied to your compensation.

An understanding of the basics of budgeting and the budget process is, therefore, essential to creating realistic budgets that will later serve as performance benchmarks. Moreover, if you are skilled at "selling the budget" within your organization and nego-tiating compromises during the budgeting process, you will be more likely to see your budget requests met.

How does the budgeting process work?

The process of preparing a budget involves establishing goals, evaluating different strategies for achieving these goals, and as-sessing the financial impacts of these strategies. There are typically four components in the budget-preparation process.

1. **Setting goals.** Some organizations mandate companywide goals, such as "Increase net profits by 10 percent during the next year." Individual departments then translate these direc-tives into financial goals that are relevant for their particular activities. For example, the sales department might set a goal of increasing revenues, while the purchasing department will look for ways to reduce costs.

2. **Evaluating and choosing options.** Several tactics—such as launching a new marketing campaign to drive sales, finding a lower-cost supplier to reduce expenses, and hiring more em-ployees to improve customer service—may be used to meet a specific goal. You will need to consider which tactics are likely

to be most effective in your particular situation and which will also be supported across the organization. After all, a great idea is just that—an idea—if you don't get approval to implement it.

3. **Identifying budget impacts.** Decisions about strategic goals and tactics are used to develop assumptions about future costs and revenues. For example, upgrading your advertising to reach more markets might mean that you need to hire professional marketing consultants.

4. **Coordinating departmental budgets.** Individual unit and division budgets are combined into a single master budget that expresses the organization's overall financial objectives and strategic goals.

Typically, preparing budgets is an iterative process in which different groups create preliminary budgets and then come together to identify and resolve differences.

Why is a budget valuable?

Budgets can serve as essential tools for measuring managers' performance. By comparing actual business results to the budget over a period of time, an evaluator can determine a manager's overall success in achieving his or her department's strategic goals.

Of course, actual results may differ from budgeted results due to reasons beyond an individual manager's control—such as an overall downturn in the economic cycle or an unexpected spike in prices of raw materials. Thus anyone using a budget to evaluate a manager's performance should be sure that the performance evaluations are matched to appropriate measures of results.

Many different financial measures of managerial performance can be drawn from comparing budgeted to actual business results. Here are a few examples:

- *Gross margin* measures profitability after direct production costs but before other costs that are not specifically tied to production, such as marketing, administrative, and interest expenses. For example:

  Gross margin = $40,000/$120,000 = 33%

- *SG&A* (selling, general, and administrative costs) as a percentage of sales is a measure of a department's or organization's effectiveness in controlling costs. For instance:

  SG&A as a percentage of sales = $20,000/$120,000 = 16.7%

- *Revenue per employee* is a measure of the operational efficiency of a department or organization, relative to other units or companies in the same industry. To illustrate:

  Revenue per employee = $120,000,000/225 = $533,333

These and other measures can help an organization evaluate the effectiveness of its managers.

Types of budgets

There are different types of budgets for different purposes. Some of the main types of budgets include the following:

- *Operating budgets* reflect day-to-day expenses and depreciation (the current portion of capitalized expenses). They typically cover a one-year period. Department, division, and unit managers are usually asked to come up with operating budgets for their part of the business.

- *Capital budgets* show planned outlays for investments in plant, equipment, and product development. Capital budgets may cover periods of three, five, or ten years. Again, managers throughout an organization may be expected to prepare this type of budget.

- *Cash budgets* plot the expected cash balances the organization will experience during the forecast period, based on information provided in operating and capital budgets. Cash budgets are prepared by an organization's finance department and are critical to ensuring that the company has sufficient liquidity (cash and credit) available to meet expected cash disbursements.

- *Master budgets* reflect the aggregation of department, division, and business unit budgets. As we've seen, department or unit managers are most frequently asked to develop operating budgets and capital budgets for their departments. You can also create subsets of the operating and capital budgets for individual projects, geographic locations, or large, line item expenses such as advertising. These detailed schedules allow you to keep a closer eye on revenues and expenses within your department. Departmental operating and capital budgets are coordinated to create *financial budgets* including the cash budget, the budgeted balance sheet, and the budgeted statement of cash flows. All of these budgets together are then "rolled up into" the master budget, summarizing the financial projections within an organization for a given period of time. See the illustration "Coordinating departmental budgets into the master budget" on page 11 for an example of how this works.

Steps for Preparing a Cash Budget

A cash budget helps ensure that your organization, division, or department will have the cash necessary to function throughout the budget period. The cash budget can be broken down into smaller units—months or quarters, for example—within the entire budget period to reflect changing cash flows.

1. **Determine the beginning cash balance.** Determine how much cash will be available at the beginning of the period (fiscal year or quarter or month).

2. **Add receipts.** Determine the expected receipts—collections from customers—that will flow into the cash account each period. Cash collections may vary during the budget period. For example, many retail stores expect to receive most of their receipts during holiday seasons.

3. **Deduct disbursements.** According to expected activity, calculate how much cash will be required to cover disbursements—cash payouts—during the period. Disbursements could include payment for materials, payroll, taxes due, and so on. Some of these expenditures may be evenly distributed throughout the budget period, but some, such as payroll or material costs, may fluctuate as part of the production process.

4. **Calculate the cash excess or deficiency.** To calculate the cash excess or deficiency for a period, subtract the disbursement from the sum of the beginning cash balance and the receipts expected during that period.

5. **Determine financing needed.** To calculate the cash excess or deficiency for a period, subtract the disbursement from total cash available. If, at the end of the period, there is a cash excess, then financing of operations may be covered by the available cash. If, on the other hand, there is a cash deficiency, then you have to plan on financing the period's cash needs from other sources, such as a bank loan. Note: remember to include a stable cash balance beyond the immediate cash needs. For example, a manufacturing division may want to maintain a $30,000 cash balance at all times to cover unexpected cash demands. When you borrow money for operating expenses, you need to establish a payback schedule. For each period, include the repayment of loan principal and interest in the cash budget.

6. **Establish the ending cash balance.** The ending cash balance for each period will include the receipts and loans less the disbursements and financing costs. The ending cash balance becomes the beginning cash balance for the next period.

Coordinating departmental budgets into the master budget

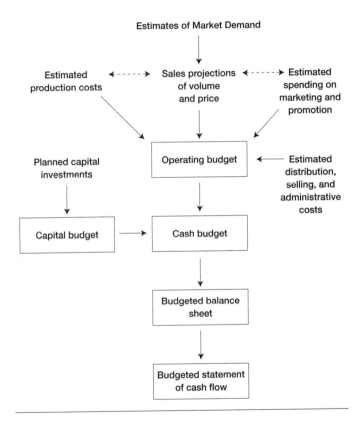

Approaches to Preparing a Budget

OW DO YOU APPROACH preparing budgets needed for your part of the organization? You have several options at your disposal. Below, we examine a few different approaches.

Traditional budgeting

Many organizations use a "traditional" budget—a budget that covers a one-year period and that presents forecasts that do not change during the life of the budget cycle. Companies use traditional budgets because they are easy to put together and they simplify coordination of budget assumptions across different departments.

Traditional budgets, however, have been under growing attack from those who feel that they no longer serve a modern organization's needs. Critics complain that such budgets are timed incorrectly (too long or too short); rely on inappropriate measures; and are too simplistic (or too complex), too rigid (inflexible in a changing business environment), or too political (the incentives for managers send the wrong messages).

As a result, some organizations blend alternative approaches to budgeting to meet their individual needs. Below, we show how the traditional approach contrasts with alternative approaches.

Alternative approaches

The table "Traditional budgets and alternative approaches" on page 17 shows the elements of a traditional budget and some alternative approaches to budgeting that your company may use.

While the alternative approaches may result in greater accuracy and functionality, they also have their disadvantages. For example, some (such as zero-based budgeting) can consume so much time that they distract managers from other critical activities.

Kaizen budgeting

If your company uses *Kaizen budgeting*, cost reductions are built into the budget on an incremental basis so that continual efforts are made to reduce costs over a given time period. The advantage of Kaizen budgeting is that the budget process puts continuous pressure on managers to achieve cost efficiencies. A disadvantage is that Kaizen budgeting is difficult to maintain because the rate of budgeted cost reduction declines over time, making it more difficult to achieve improvements after the "easy" changes have been achieved.

Budgeting and the balanced scorecard

For the most part, traditional budgeting has focused on the financial performance of an organization. However, many of these financial performance measures, designed to indicate the success of budget plans in contributing to increasing profits, were developed for an industrial world.

What Would YOU Do?

Feeding the Dragon

MEI PO RUNS Gift of the Dragon, a small artisan shop that makes decorations and gifts for the Chinese New Year. Unique handcrafted touches and a great word-of-mouth reputation keep her products in high demand.

Recently, Mei Po learned that the space next door was available to lease. The timing was right as she was looking to expand her business. But as she reviewed the loan application, she noticed that in addition to a business plan, she needed to prepare a one-year budget. Mei Po was taken aback.

She planned her cash flow month to month. How could she predict what would happen over the period of a year? It seemed impossible. She wondered where to even start.

What would YOU do? The mentors will suggest a solution in *What You COULD Do.*

Times have changed, and new ways of approaching planning and performance evaluation have changed as well. With information technology and global markets becoming the model for the modern business environment, and as nonprofit organizations grow in size and sophistication, organizations have to recognize

Traditional budgets and alternative approaches

Budget parameter	Approach	Description
Time period of the budget	Fixed budget (traditional)	The budget period is a specific time period, usually coinciding with the company's fiscal year.
	Rolling budget	The budget is continuously updated so that the time frame remains stable while the actual period covered by the budget changes. For example, as each month passes, a one-year rolling budget would be extended by one month so that there would always be a one-year budget in place.
Forecast values	Static budget (traditional)	Presents one forecast for a given time period and is not changed during the life of the budget.
	Flexible budget	Budgeted revenues and costs are adjusted during the budget period according to predetermined variances between the budgeted and actual output and revenue.
Forecasting process	Incremental budgeting (traditional)	The previous period's budget and actual results, as well as expectations for the future, are used in determining the budget for the next period.
	Zero-based budgeting	The budgeting process begins from the ground up, as though the budget were being prepared for the first time.
Setting goals	Top-down budgeting (traditional)	Senior management sets budget goals—such as revenue and profit—and imposes these goals on the rest of the organization.
	Participatory budgeting	Those responsible for achieving the budget goals are included in setting those goals.

and value their intangible and intellectual assets as well as the tangible assets represented in numbers on the balance sheet.

The *balanced scorecard* is a way for managers to view their organization from four interrelated perspectives of operational drivers for future performance:

1. **Financial perspective.** How are we doing using traditional financial performance measures? How do shareholders view us?

2. **Customer perspective.** How satisfied, loyal, and profitable are our customers?

3. **Internal process perspective.** What internal business processes do we excel at, and which processes do we need to improve?

4. **Learning and growth perspective.** How can we build a workforce that is constantly learning and improving, so that employees excel at their jobs in ways that delight customers and generate the financial results our company needs?

The balanced scorecard gives upper management a quick and effective view of the critical factors affecting the organization's performance now and in the future. The methodology also puts the strategic mission, rather than financial controls, at the center of the budget-preparation process.

The balanced scorecard is linked to the budget process in the following ways:

- It highlights leading indicators, such as new product development, customer complaints, or direct mail response rates, instead of only sales or cost figures.

- It balances the four perspectives. Thus, for example, pressure to develop new products doesn't overshadow the need for quality products and customer satisfaction.

- It helps management to communicate strategic goals and the organization's mission to all the stakeholders in the enterprise.

To build a balanced scorecard, managers follow these steps:

- **Develop goals and measures for critical financial performance measures.** In other words, prepare a budget as a financial action plan.

- **Develop goals and measures for critical customer performance variables.** Managers first identify the target market, and then they develop ways to measure variables such as customer loyalty through repeat buying, response rates, new customer referrals, customer complaints, and price sensitivity. The focus is on identifying ways to retain current customers, increase levels of customer purchases, increase levels of profitability per customer, and acquire new customers.

- **Develop goals and measures for critical internal process performance variables.** Managers look at the three areas of internal process:

  1. The innovation cycle or research, development, and design of products and service

  2. The operations cycle in which the products are manufactured and delivered or services are rendered

3. The postsale service cycle in which customer service is the primary activity

   Each of these internal process areas relates directly to both financial performance and customer satisfaction.

- **Develop goals and measures for critical learning, and growth performance measures.** Here managers step back to consider the infrastructure and capabilities needed for the organization to create the long-term growth the strategic mission envisions. Growth will occur through human resources, systems, and organizational procedures. This perspective clarifies the investment decisions management has to make to achieve its goals. Will the organization have to invest in training people? In hiring more people for specific roles? In improving its technology systems? Empowering employees—encouraging employee loyalty—and aligning organizational structures to meet the company's changing needs simultaneously enhance the ability of the organization in the other three critical areas.

The key to linking the balanced scorecard is to develop the performance measures or drivers that can help predict future outcomes. The balanced scorecard provides the guidance for planning—the budget—which, in turn, provides feedback and allows for course correction as the time period stipulated in the budget advances. This provides information managers can use to translate the strategic vision into reality and to constanty improve the budget-preparation process.

What You COULD Do.

Remember Mei Po's concern about how to begin preparing her one-year budget?

Here's what the mentor suggests:

The first step in developing a budget is to establish a set of assumptions about the future. Questions Mei Po might ask include, Will the demand for her gifts grow over the next year? If yes, by how much? The next step is for Mei Po to calculate expected revenues and expenses based on past performance and future expectations. The difference between revenues and expenses is net income. If Mei Po is satisfied with the numbers, she can finalize her budget. If she wants higher net income, she needs to identify new strategies that will support different assumptions.

Categorizing Expenses

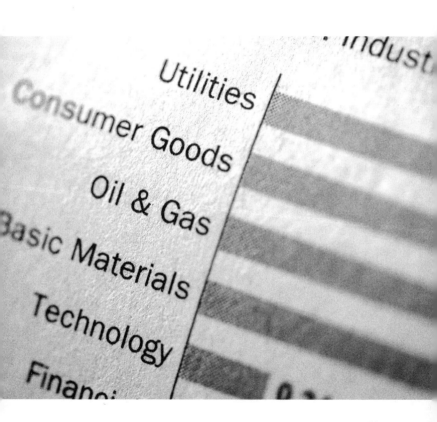

A BIG PART OF preparing any budget is anticipating and categorizing various types of expenses. Below are some suggestions for making sure you've covered all the bases when it comes to expenses for your department or unit.

Fixed and variable costs

In preparing budgets, you need to differentiate between fixed costs and variable costs. *Fixed costs* are those that remain fairly constant within a wide range of production or sales volumes. Examples of fixed costs include:

- Rent
- Basic utilities, including electric and telephone service
- Equipment leases
- Depreciation
- Interest payments
- Administrative costs
- Marketing and advertising
- Indirect labor, such as salaried supervisory employees

Variable costs are those that change in direct proportion to changes in activity. Examples of variable costs include:

- Raw materials

- Direct labor

- Packaging

- Depreciation due to usage

- Power and gas used in manufacturing

- Shipping

- Sales commissions

- Income taxes

Estimates of variable costs that will be incurred during the budget period will depend on the production forecast you come up with for your unit or department. On the surface some costs may appear fixed. In reality, however, they represent long-term variable costs. For example, if production or sales volumes increase by a sufficiently large amount, a company may need to lease additional equipment, rent more warehouse space, or hire additional administrative help. Being aware of such requirements will enable you to anticipate the need for expanded capacity and to include these expenditures in your budget requests.

Allocated costs

Operating budgets may include *allocated costs*—costs associated with operating the overall company that are not tied to individual products or departments. The most significant allocation is usually overhead. This figure typically includes the office rent for the

What Would YOU Do?

Smooth Operator?

ELKE HAS RECENTLY become manager of the shoe division of LifeSport, a sportswear manufacturing company. Today, she and LifeSport's other division managers are meeting with their boss, Ahmed, to begin planning next year's division budgets.

During the meeting, Ahmed states LifeSport's strategic goals for next year. "Our industry has been quite stable," he says. "For this year, I'd like to see if all our divisions can boost their operating income by 10 percent, without increasing costs any more than they have to." Ahmed then encourages the managers to use the budget-preparation experience to deepen their understanding of marketplace realities.

Elke returns to her office, thinking about what approach she should take to creating a budget that achieves Ahmed's strategic goals. Should she take last year's operating income for her division and project the desired 10 percent increase for the upcoming year? What about creating a plan that calls for monthly (rather than quarterly) reviews and updates to the budget, so she can react to marketplace realities? Should she instead ask various managers throughout LifeSport what market trends they expect to see next year? It all seems so complicated.

What would YOU do? The mentors will suggest a solution in *What You COULD Do*.

building occupied by corporate headquarters, and salaries and expenses associated with corporate management.

How these costs are attributed to individual departments varies from one company to another. Some organizations may allocate overhead to certain department budgets—those that produce revenue, for example—and not others.

Activity-based costing

Your company may use *activity-based costing (ABC)* to allocate costs. Activity-based costing allows companies to more precisely identify overhead costs associated with producing revenue. Instead of allocating overhead costs to products based on broad measures such as revenue or production volume, ABC starts with the cost of resources, allocates these costs to activities, and then allocates the cost of activities to products. Activities may be broadly defined (such as managing purchasing) or narrowly defined (such as managing purchasing for research and development). Maintaining an ABC system requires managers and employees to gather detailed information about how much of their time is devoted to particular activities.

Activity-based budgeting

Organizations that use ABC to allocate overhead and other costs to individual departments may also adopt *activity-based budgeting (ABB)*. Activity-based budgeting starts with forecasting the planned sales volume for each product. Historical data from the activity-based costing system is then used to estimate the required activities to produce that volume, the resources required to support those activities, and the cost of those resources. The illustration "Inverse relationship between ABC and ABB" shows an example.

Inverse relationship between ABC and ABB

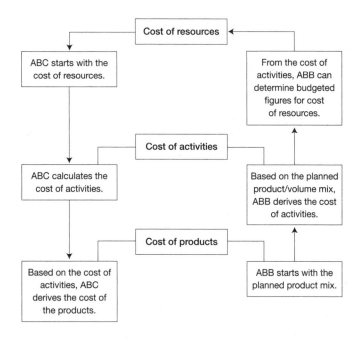

Source: Adapted from Robert S. Kaplan and Robin Cooper, *Cost and Effect: Using Integrated Cost Systems to Drive Profitability and Performance* (Boston: Harvard Business School Press, 1998).

The primary advantage of activity-based budgets is that costs can be more accurately associated with activities, making the planning process more precise and corrections more effective. Companies using this approach report benefits including:

- Establishing more realistic budgets

- Improved accuracy in identifying resource needs

- Better linking of costs to outputs

- More precise allocation of costs to staff responsibilities

The disadvantage of this approach is that it can be costly and complex to establish. Thus it may not be worth the trouble for a small company with few products or services. It also has to be adopted by and embedded into the whole organization; one division alone can't decide to develop its own ABC or ABB system. But when the circumstances are right, activity-based approaches to understanding the economic dynamics of an organization provide long-term planning benefits.

What You COULD Do.

Remember Elke's uncertainty about how to prepare an operating budget for her division that supports the company's new strategic goal?

Here's what the mentor suggests:

Elke should start by asking the finance manager, purchasing group, and other managers throughout LifeSport what market trends they expect to see next year. It's valuable to begin the process of preparing any budget by making *assumptions* about the future. For example, Elke will need to estimate whether the market will grow next year, how customers will respond to new products or features, and what competitors will be doing. Then she'll have to make projections about revenues and other budget figures for her division based on that data.

To establish these assumptions, she should gather information from the financial group (they have estimates of future economic trends), human resources (they understand labor market shifts), sales reps (they know consumer trends), and purchasing (they have news about suppliers).

This is a far better step than taking last year's operating income for her division and merely projecting the desired 10 percent increase for the coming year. Though many companies use historical figures to extrapolate subsequent budgets, this approach doesn't encourage managers to evaluate the realities of the current and future marketplace—something Ahmed stressed during the meeting. Also, it encourages some managers to develop a "use it or lose it" point of view. They feel they must use all of their budgeted expenditures by the end of the period so the next period's budget won't be reduced by the amount that would have been saved.

Preparing an Operating Budget

N OW LET'S TURN to how you might prepare an operating budget for your department or unit. To prepare such a budget, you need to take eight steps:

- Defining your goals
- Articulating your assumptions
- Forecasting sales
- Forecasting revenues
- Forecasting cost of goods sold
- Estimating SG&A costs
- Calculating operating income
- Exploring "what-if" scenarios

Below, we look at each of these steps more closely.

Defining your goals

Some goals may be set by senior management, while others are determined by the managers of individual departments or units. These goals will reflect both the organization's larger strategic priorities and the department's or business unit's tactical goals. Examples of questions you might ask to help define your department's tactical goals include:

- What technological changes are affecting our industry?

- How can our current business processes be improved?

- What longer-term initiatives should we consider in order to position our company to compete successfully in the future?

Achieving these goals requires choosing tactics that may in turn affect the budget. The table "Examples of goals, options, and budget impacts" provides an illustration.

Examples of goals, options, and budget impacts

Goal	Options	Budget impacts
Become the most reliable provider of Internet services	Maintain state-of-the-art equipment	Capital investment
	Train the most skilled repair teams in the field	Higher labor and training costs
	Provide the most timely customer service	Increased spending on customer support
Increase revenues by 10%	Raise prices	Lower sales volume, higher gross margin
	Expand marketing	Increased sales, higher marketing costs, increased production costs
	Enter into partnerships	Increased revenues, higher production costs, higher selling costs

What Would YOU Do?

No Day at the Beach

IT'S NOVEMBER. And Jorge is under pressure. He's trying to forecast next year's sales at his Los Angeles–based beach ball company, Beachy Keen. This past year was rough. El Nino (the seasonal warming of the tide) caused larger-than-usual waves in southern California. People filled amusement parks instead of beaches. Luckily, next year's weather is predicted to be back to normal—and Jorge plans to seize the opportunity to launch a new marketing campaign.

He mulls over what data he should use to forecast next year's sales. First, he considers using the run rate. He also evaluates the potential of using the past year's projected annual sales. And he weights the possibility of using the past year's projected annual sales plus 25 percent. Each option seems to offer valuable information, so he's not sure what to do.

What would YOU do? The mentors will suggest a solution in *What You COULD Do.*

Articulating your assumptions

Whenever you prepare a budget, you have to make some assumptions about the future. In many companies, senior management will communicate key assumptions that are to be used throughout the organization—such as a 5 percent increase in salaries or a 10 percent increase in sales volumes. In other cases, the assumptions are specific to each department's activities.

Managers use a wide variety of data and approaches to articulate their assumptions, including historical trends, purchasing surveys, and industry projections. They also communicate with each other about their expectations for customer response, supplier performance, financial market fluctuation, and so on. Be sure to document all of your assumptions, and keep notes of sources of information you use.

"Unless we find some way to keep our sights on tomorrow, we cannot expect to be in touch with today."
—Dean Rusk

Tips for Setting Assumptions

- Use historical data as a starting point. Even when times are changing quickly, information about past performance can establish a base from which to begin.
- Trust your own experience. Make educated guesses about what is likely to happen in the future.
- Listen to your intuition. Even though you can't verify those gut feelings, you can take them into account.
- Do due diligence. Go out and get the information you need. This may involve doing research, reading trade journals, collecting industry statistics, and so on. And don't forget that the Internet is a growing information resource.

- Talk with and listen to knowledgeable people. Discuss your ideas with team members, colleagues, mentors. Seek out industry participants, suppliers, concerned community leaders, and experts in the field. Engage in discussions with competitors.
- Learn when to be a risk taker and when to be conservative. In a volatile market, conservative assumptions may be the safest.
- Test your assumptions. If possible, try out your assumptions in small experiments before you accept them.

Forecasting sales

Sales projections for a given period are developed by product or product group. If you are forecasting product sales, consider whether it is appropriate to base your forecasts on current sales trends. Some factors to consider, in addition to overall demand trends for these types of products, are:

- The history of sales growth for your company's products

- Competitive products that have been or may be introduced in the market

- Availability of substitute products (for example, if your company sells carbonated beverages, tea and coffee may be substitute products)

- Price sensitivity of purchasers (that is, will a slight increase in price drive customers away?)

- Percentage of customers who make repeat purchases

- Planned changes in sales and promotion activities

If you use historical sales data as a base for your sales forecasts, determine whether it is appropriate to use annual data or the run rate.

The *run rate* is the extrapolation of current financial results out over a future period of time. For example, if December's sales are $75,000, the annual run rate ($75,000 multiplied by twelve months) is $900,000.

Annual data may be most appropriate for forecasting one-off product sales, while the run rate may be better if you are forecasting revenues for services sold under long-term contracts or for recently launched products.

In the examples on the two next pages, the company sells products and also sells monthly services under long-term contracts. The table "Forecasting revenues using the run rate for product and contract sales" shows projected sales for year 2 using the run rate from year 1. The table "Forecasting revenues at 110 percent of total year 1 product and contract sales" shows projected sales for year 2 assuming a 10 percent increase over total sales from year 1.

For products, the examples assume that sales are fairly evenly distributed over the course of year 1, so there is little difference between the two approaches ($900,000 versus $965,800). However, if product sales were concentrated in only a few months of the year, using the run rate would grossly over- or underestimate product revenues for year 2.

Forecasting revenues using the run rate for product and contract sales

	Dec. year 1 sales	Year 2 total projected sales @ Dec. year 1 run rate
Product sales	$75,000	$900,000
Contract monthly services sales:		
Client A (added Jan. year 1)	$4,000	$48,000
Client B (added Apr. year 1)	$4,000	$48,000
Client C (added Oct. year 1)	$6,000	$72,000
Client D (added Dec. year 1)	$9,000	$108,000
Subtotal contract services sales:	**$23,000**	**$276,000**
Total revenue:	$98,000	$1,176,000

Projections for contract services in the example are more realistic when the run rate is used ($276,000) because many new contracts signed in year 1 were signed late in the year. Using annual data for contract services results in a very conservative estimate ($122,100) for year 2.

The most realistic revenue forecast for this company, and the revenue figure that will be used in subsequent examples, is $1,241,800. This amount is based on 110 percent of year 1 product sales, plus the December run rate for contract services.

Forecasting revenues at 110 percent of total year 1 product and contract sales

	Year 1 total sales	Year 2 total projected sales @ 110% of year 1 total sales
Product sales	$878,000	$965,800
Contract monthly services sales:		
Client A (added Jan. year 1)	$48,000	$52,800
Client B (added Apr. year 1)	$36,000	$39,600
Client C (added Oct. year 1)	$18,000	$19,800
Client D (added Dec. year 1)	$9,000	$9,900
Subtotal contract services sales:	**$111,000**	**$122,100**
Total revenue:	$939,000	$1,087,900

Forecasting revenues

Historical data, existing order backlogs, and information about the sales pipeline can help you estimate how new sales volume might be distributed during the budget period. If necessary, create a monthly schedule to clarify how sales volumes and revenues are expected to fluctuate during the year. Doing so will help prevent overly optimistic forecasts. This is important, because it's all too easy to let overoptimism distort your forecasts. David Michels, former group chief executive of the Hilton Group, offered some valuable insights into this issue:

> *One of the strangest things that I've encountered in all the businesses I've been in, and ever since I've been in business, is that I can rarely remember anyone—whether it's in betting hotels, holiday camps, bingo or machine sales—ever bringing me a five-year forecast (which is what most people ask for) where business wasn't always better in the fifth year.*
>
> *What you normally get, which is quite infamous, is the wonderful "hockey stick" forecast, where perhaps business isn't wonderful now so the graph comes down a bit. Then for the next four years it goes up, and the ending is always Y percentage higher than the beginning. First, one needs to understand why people do that. You're presenting something that might be your own job, your own idea, your own division, your own department or your own business to your boss or a committee of bosses. Very few people want to sit in front of them saying: "OK chaps, I'm going to do much worse in five years than I am now. Can I have a raise?" So, it's very important to remember that.*
>
> *The other thing is that people are natural optimists: really, most of us are. If you ask people "Will the weather be better next month than it is this month?" nine out of ten people will tell you "yes," because they want it to be—not because they necessarily believe it will be.*

And if you ask: "Will business be better next month or in five years' time?" most people will say "Yes"; not because they believe it will be but because they want it to be. It's just natural human emotion.

Since revenues are a function of units sold and price, you will want to document quantity and price assumptions used in developing your revenue forecast. Be aware that production constraints may affect the revenue budget. If, for example, you expect sales demand to exceed capacity, then you'll need to adjust the revenue budget to match the production constraints rather than the actual demands of the market.

Be prepared to defend your assumptions, especially if you are also evaluated based on achieving your budgeted revenue targets.

Forecasting cost of goods sold

After defining your goals, articulating your assumptions, and forecasting sales and revenues, the next step in preparing your operating budget is to estimate costs associated with those revenues. One of those is the cost of goods sold.

These costs include materials, labor, other direct product costs, and manufacturing overhead. You estimate them based on units of product or, for a service company, hours of service. In forecasting cost of goods sold, consider the expected sales volume as well as planned changes in inventory. For example, if inventories are depleted at the beginning of the budget period, additional production will be required to bring inventories up to normal levels,

Cost of goods sold: year 2 budget

	Actual Year 1	Year 2 budget	Rate of change
Cost of goods sold:			
Direct labor	$192,325	$256,500	33.4%
Overhead	$6,755	$7,200	7.0%
Direct materials	$111,000	$119,000	7.2%
Total cost of goods sold	**$310,080**	**$382,700**	**23.4%**

increasing total direct production costs. Conversely, excess inventory will be worked off during the period, reducing forecast production costs.

In estimating line item expenses, be aware of breakpoints in production capacity that signal the need for additional outlays. For example, suppose you currently need three people to produce ten thousand orders a month, and you estimate that during the next year sales will increase by 20 percent to twelve thousand orders. At what point will you need to add additional staff to handle the extra volume? The table "Cost of goods sold: year 2 budget" shows one possible response.

Estimating SG&A costs

Selling, general, and administrative costs are additional costs associated with revenues. They can include costs generated by research and development, product design, marketing, distribution, cus-

SG&A: year 2 budget

	Actual Year 1	Year 2 budget	Rate of change
Sales, general, and administrative costs:			
Sales salaries	$220,000	$291,200	32.4%
Advertising expenses	$45,000	$51,000	13.3%
Miscellaneous selling expenses	$4,200	$3,900	(7.1%)
Office expenses	$92,000	$94,500	2.7%
Total SG&A	**$361,200**	**$440,600**	**22.0%**

tomer service, commissions, administration, and overhead. In the example shown in the table "SG&A: year 2 budget," only marketing and administrative expenses make up the SG&A budget.

Calculating operating income

Now it's time to calculate *operating income*—the difference between expected sales and expected costs—for your budget. The table "Operating income: year 2 budget" shows an example.

In this sample budget, contract service sales resulted in a significant jump in anticipated sales revenues in year 2. However, sales salaries and direct labor costs rose in proportion. The projected growth in operating income is largely due to the assumption that overhead and direct materials costs would not be affected by the increase in contract sales.

Operating income: year 2 budget

	Actual Year 1	Year 2 budget	Rate of change
Operating income:			
Total revenue	**$939,000**	**$1,241,800**	**32.2%**
Cost of goods sold	$310,080	$382,700	23.4%
SG&A	$361,200	$440,600	22.0%
Total costs	**$92,000**	**$94,500**	**22.6%**
Total operating income	**$671,280**	**$823,300**	**56.3%**

Exploring "what-if" scenarios

You'll probably have to rework the first draft of your operating budget in order to bring the budgeted results in line with your company's and department's goals and constraints. Testing different possible scenarios can help you with this part of the process. How will a change in one area affect the expected outcome? What if we increase advertising? How much would that increase sales? What if employees decide to go on strike? How can we incorporate that risk into the budget?

A budget is an action plan based on the best available information and assumptions for the future. Performing a sensitivity analysis to test those assumptions or alternative options can greatly enhance the value of budgets as tools for planning and for feedback and course correction.

A sensitivity analysis applies a "what-if" situation to the budget model to see the effect of a potential change on the original data.

For example, what if the cost of materials rises 5 percent, or what if sales rise 10 percent? Calculations for sensitivity analysis can be complicated when dealing with a master budget that has summarized multiple divisional and/or functional budgets. Software packages for financial planning models are available and commonly used to perform these calculations, giving managers a powerful tool to determine the costs and benefits of various options and possibilities.

Using scenario analysis software, you can quickly see the potential impact of a change in assumptions, without having to generate new forecasts for each budget item, such as raw materials or selling and administrative costs. The table "Example of sensitivity analysis" shows how sensitivity analyses for one company might be reported.

Example of sensitivity analysis

What-if scenario	Units sold	Direct materials cost	Operating income
Budget	**21,400**	**$214,000**	**$383,950**
Scenario 1: increase unit sales 10%:	23,540	$203,300	$360,900
Scenario 2: decrease unit sales 5%:	20,330	$6,000	$6,000
Scenario 3: decrease materials cost 5%:	21,400	$203,300	$398,700

Tips for Negotiating Your Team's Budget

- Make sure you understand your organization's budgeting process. What are the guidelines you need to follow? What is the timing of the budget process? How is the budget used in the organization?

- Communicate often with the controller or finance person in your department. Ask questions about points you don't understand. Get that person's advice about the assumptions your team is making.

- Know what real concerns are driving the people making the decisions about your budget. Then be sure to address those concerns.

- Get buy-in from the decision makers. Spend time educating the finance person or decision maker about your area of the business. That will lay the groundwork for implementing changes later.

- Understand each line item in the budget you're working on. If you don't know what something means or where a number comes from, find out yourself. Walk the floor. Talk to people on the line.

- Have an ongoing discussion with your team throughout the budget period. The more you plan, the more you will be able to respond to unplanned contingencies.

- Avoid unpleasant surprises! As they become available, compare actual figures to the budgeted amounts. If there is a significant or unexpected variance, find out why. And be sure to notify the finance person who needs to know.

What You COULD Do.

Remember Jorge's uncertainty about which data he should use to forecast next year's sales at Beachy Keen?

Here's what the mentor suggests:

Jorge should use the past year's projected annual sales plus 25 percent. That's because El Nino caused poor beach conditions and low sales this past year, so higher sales are a reasonable projection for next year. In addition, his new marketing campaign will likely increase revenues.

Using the run rate wouldn't be appropriate in this case. Because beach ball sales are seasonal, using any single month as a base for projections will yield a result that is either too high or too low. Using the past year's projected annual sales would also be an unwise move—again, because El Nino caused poor beach conditions and low sales in the previous year, making higher sales a reasonable projection for next year.

Preparing a Capital Budget

I N ADDITION TO preparing operating budgets for your department or unit, you may need to prepare capital budgets. Let's now examine this type of budget more carefully and consider strategies for preparing one.

What is a capital budget?

A *capital budget* is a schedule that shows planned investments in property, equipment, improvements, and other capital assets over a period of time. These outlays are different from ordinary day-to-day expenses in that they can be capitalized under accepted accounting practices. Instead of having to record the entire expense as a deduction from income in one accounting period, you can spread the capitalized expense out over a period of years. Each year, a portion of the capitalized expense is recorded as depreciation.

If you are asked to submit a capital budget request, you will need to estimate the total expenditure associated with each type of investment. For example, you might have one line item for computers, one for office equipment, and another for furniture. Your budget should also include amounts for related costs such as installation charges, consulting fees, the cost of permits, or service contracts.

A capital budget may show planned investments over several years. The table "Example of a capital budget" illustrates a capital

Example of a capital budget

	Year 1	Year 2	Year 3
IT equipment:			
Computers	$45,000	$15,000	$15,000
Servers	$120,000	$25,000	$25,000
Support service	$26,000	–	$29,000
Furniture and fixtures:			
Office furniture	$28,000	$6,000	$6,000
Renovation costs	$89,000	–	–

budget for a department that is migrating to a new computer system in year 1. The budget shows migration costs expected to be incurred in year 1, and estimated costs in subsequent years based on projected growth.

Capital budgeting techniques

Capital budgeting is slightly different from a capital budget—despite the similarity of the terms! It's the process of identifying the potential return on a given investment to determine whether the investment makes sense and to compare alternative investment options. Capital budgeting thus is a key step in preparing a capital budget.

If many different departments are competing to have projects funded, you may be asked to justify your proposals using capital budgeting techniques. The following steps can help:

1. Prepare a schedule of estimated cash flows that identifies outlays, the timing of those outlays, and the expected cost savings or revenue that will result from the investment. For substantial investments, consider annual cash flows over a period of several years. If an expense will be capitalized, the full outlay is recorded for the year in which it is incurred. Also record the expected tax savings that will result in subsequent years as capitalized items are depreciated.

2. Calculate the *net present value* (NPV) of the cash flows using appropriate interest rates. Net present value is the current value of future cash flows. You calculate it by dividing each future cash flow by the compounded interest rate and then adding up all of the discounted cash flows. You can create a spreadsheet (for situations where cash flows or the interest rates used are different from year to year) or use a financial calculator (if the cash flow and interest rate are constant throughout the period).

The NPV formula is:

$$\text{Net present value} = \text{Cash flow}\,(CF) + \frac{CF_1}{(1+i)^1} + \frac{CF_2}{(1+i)^2} + \frac{CF_n}{(1+i)^2}$$

where each *CF* is a future cash flow, *n* is the number of years over which the cash flow is expected to occur, and *i* is the interest rate.

Some experts suggest that the interest rate should be based on the company's cost of capital, while others recommend using a risk-adjusted rate that reflects the uncertainty of the future cash flows. Check with your manager to find out how your company handles this.

3. A positive net present value indicates that the investment will potentially benefit the company, while a negative net present value indicates a losing proposition.

When Your Budget and Reality Differ

BECAUSE ALL BUDGETS are based on assumptions about what might happen in the future, actual business results for the future time period stipulated in a particular budget may not reflect what was in the budget. Below are some insights into how you might respond to this situation.

What is variance?

The difference between the actual results produced by your department or unit and the budgeted results you've planned for is called the *variance*. Comparison of actual to budgeted results allows you to consider whether corrective action is needed. The variance can be favorable, when the actual results are better than expected. For example, sales increase more than you anticipated. Or it can be unfavorable, when the actual results are worse than expected. For instance, sales increase less than you anticipated.

Unfavorable variances require corrective action so that future results will be closer to budget. To illustrate, if the increase in sales was less than you had budgeted, you would want to find out why and then address the problem. Was it that salespeople lacked sufficient training in the new products your company was trying to sell? If so, perhaps your department could provide the needed training.

If you cannot affect a particular expense or revenue item, you may be able to compensate by taking action that will cause an offsetting variance in other budget line items. That is, if you have to live with a less-than-ideal increase in sales, perhaps you could cut costs in another area, so that your department's *overall* performance is still good in financial terms.

What causes it?

Sometimes variances are artificially created. For example, if the company's accounting software automatically spreads line item expenses over a twelve-month period and the actual expenditure only occurs once a year, you will have a favorable variance in some months and an unfavorable variance in others.

The table "Possible causes of variance and possible responses" shows examples.

Possible causes of variance and possible responses

Variance	Possible causes	Compensating action
Higher production costs	Increased production volume	None required if increase in production is due to increased sales
	Increase in price of raw materials or labor	Increase selling prices, reduce other expenses
	Timing differences create artificial variance	None required
Lower revenues	Fewer units sold	Reduce fixed expenses and/or increase promotion activities
	Lower selling prices	Reduce expenses or increase selling prices

Tips and Tools

Tools for
Preparing a Budget

Budget Preparation and Tracking

Use this worksheet to prepare and track an annual budget needed for your department, division, or business unit.

	Q1 budget	Q1 actual	Q2 budget	Q2 actual	Q3 budget	Q4 actual	Q4 budget	Q4 actual	YTD budget	YTD actual	YTD difference	YTD % difference
Revenues (list sources on separate lines)												
Total revenues												
Expenses (list items on separate lines)												
Total expenses												
Operating income as a % of revenue												
Submitted by:												
Date updated:												

Budget Preparation Checklist

Use this form to identify sources of information for your budget. You can change the items listed to fit your situation, such as a service business or start-up company.

Revenue *Do you have information from or about:*

☐ Senior management, goals and objectives, strategy, mission

☐ Sales and marketing managers' projections, marketplace data, goals

☐ Current levels of sales

☐ Incremental changes

☐ Industry predictions/expectations, trends

☐ Field sales representatives' projections, marketplace data, assessment of competition

☐ Other: for example, new technology's impact

Production Costs *Do you have information from or about:*

Direct Materials

Current Costs

☐ Incremental change

☐ Suppliers; their predictability to deliver

☐ Purchasers estimates/expectations

☐ Industry predictions

Direct Labor

☐ Contractual changes

☐ Expected outsourcing

☐ Expected contract changes

☐ Expected overtime

☐ Changing requirements

☐ Human resource predictions

Direct Manufacturing

Variable Costs

☐ Supplies

☐ Maintenance

☐ Power

Fixed Costs

☐ Depreciation

☐ Property taxes

☐ Insurance

☐ Supervision

Continued

Do you have information from or about:

☐ Incremental change   ☐ Purchasers estimates/expectations
☐ Suppliers' estimates/expected   ☐ Industry predictions
    changes

Nonproduction Costs   *Do you have information from or about:*

Variable Costs

☐ R&D/product design   ☐ Customer Service   ☐ Distribution
☐ Marketing/Advertising   ☐ Administration

Fixed Costs

☐ R&D/product design   ☐ Customer Service   ☐ Distribution
☐ Marketing/Advertising   ☐ Administration

Do you have information from or about:

☐ Incremental change   ☐ Purchasers estimates/expectations
☐ Suppliers' estimates/expected   ☐ Industry predictions
    changes

Cash Budget

Use this worksheet to calculate your cash requirements by quarter.
Enter your detailed estimates of cash receipts and disbursements
in the spaces provided, or add new lines.

Cash Budget for Fiscal Year

	Quarters				Year Totals
	1	2	3	4	
Cash balance, beginning					
Add receipts					
Cash sales					
Collections from accounts receivable					
Investment income					
Total cash available for needs (*a*)					
Deduct disbursements					
Direct materials					
Payroll					
Income taxes					
Other costs					
Machinery purchase					
Total disbursements (cash needed) (*b*)					
Cash excess (deficiency) (a) − (b)					
Financing					
Borrowing (at beginning)					
Repayment (at end)					
Interest on borrowing					
Total effects of financing (*d*)					
Cash balance, ending (a) − (b) + (d)					

Test Yourself

This section offers ten multiple-choice questions to help you identify your baseline knowledge of the essentials of preparing a budget. Answers to the questions are given at the end of the test.

1. Which of the following is *not* a true statement?

  a. A budget is an action plan for allocating resources and expenditures.

  b. A budget is a historical record of a company's financial results.

  c. A budget is a yardstick for measuring managers' performance.

2. The most important element of the budget-preparation process is:

  a. The assessment of variances between expected and actual results.

  b. The communication and planning that occur in preparing a budget.

  c. The end result—the operating, capital, or cash budget that is created.

3. One significant disadvantage associated with zero-based budgeting is:

a. Its in-depth analysis.

b. Its overall inaccuracy.

c. Its time costs.

4. An expense that stays the same when there is an increase in the volume of product produced is categorized as a:

a. Fixed cost.

b. Variable cost.

c. Constant cost.

5. Your company's marketing department is forecasting a 15 percent increase in sales revenue next year. What assumptions should you, the production department manager, make from this forecast as you prepare your budget for next year?

a. Sales volume will increase 15 percent.

b. No assumptions can be made from this forecast.

c. Sales volume will remain the same next year.

6. It is October 1, and your department's year-to-date revenue is 20 percent less than what you had budgeted year-to-date. The run rate has jumped sharply since July, while your total expenses are right on budget. One-half of your annual bonus depends on achieving budgeted revenues by the end of the year and one-half on achieving budgeted gross margin. What action should you take?

   a. Reduce prices and increase spending on advertising and marketing.

   b. Increase prices as well as spending on advertising and marketing.

   c. Examine expense items to see whether there are any adjustments to spending you should make.

7. Capital budgeting is the process of:

   a. Identifying the potential return on a given investment to determine whether the investment makes sense and to compare alternative investment options.

   b. Estimating future outlays for property, equipment, and capital assets.

   c. Plotting the expected cash balances that the organization will experience during the forecast period.

8. You want to determine the potential impact on your division's operating income if the number of product units sold increases by 10 percent, if the number of product units sold decreases by

5 percent, and if material costs decrease by 5 percent. What would you do?

    a. Estimate costs associated with expected revenues (the cost of goods sold and the estimated SG&A), and calculate expected operating income.

    b. Differentiate between fixed and variable costs, and then allocate costs using activity-based costing (ABC).

    c. Conduct a sensitivity analysis comparing the units sold, material costs, and operating income shown in your budget against those you would see under the three proposed scenarios.

9. Which of the following goals might be appropriate for the vice president of purchasing?

    a. Reduce material costs by 15 percent.

    b. Reduce overhead by 10 percent.

    c. Increase sales revenue by 10 percent.

10. True or false: the balanced scorecard is linked to the budget process by highlighting the financial results that the company intends to achieve through its competitive strategy.

    a. True.

    b. False.

Answers to test questions

1, b. A budget is *not* a historical document but rather a forward-looking action plan that guides managers' allocation of resources and expenditures based on their assumptions about the future.

2, b. The planning and communication activities that take place in formulating a budget require managers to consider longer-term goals, challenges, and opportunities facing the organization—all of which shape major decisions about how to respond.

3, c. One problem that occurs with zero-based budgeting is that the time involved in the budget-preparation process can overwhelm planners, making implementation difficult. Managers have to balance the need for increased accuracy with the time required to collect further information.

4, a. Fixed costs, such as rent, administrative costs, and insurance, do not vary with incremental changes in production volumes.

5, b. Before you can make assumptions that inform your own budget, you must identify the assumptions behind the marketing department's revenue forecast. For example, the marketing manager may assume that the projected growth in revenue will come from a lower selling price and a dramatic increase in volume; a higher selling price and a decline in the number of units sold; or a jump in sales volume due to other factors, such as increased spending on advertising. Each of these assumptions will have different implications for your budget. Only after you've clarified marketing's assumptions can you then begin preparing your own budget.

6, c. The rising run rate indicates that sales are increasing. And if this continues, sales may come in on budget by the end of the year. The greater risk, and one over which you have more control, is that you will not meet the budgeted gross margin unless you reduce expenses to match the shortfall in revenue.

7, a. Capital budgeting involves evaluating the financial sound-ness of a proposed capital investment and choosing among alternatives.

8, c. A sensitivity analysis applies a "what-if" situation to the budget model to see the effect of the potential change on the orig-inal data. Using sensitivity analysis, you can see the possible im-pact of a change in your assumptions, without having to generate new forecasts for each budget item, such as raw materials.

9, a. The purchasing department can make a significant contri-bution to reducing materials costs by controlling what the com-pany pays for raw materials, and packaging.

10, b. The balanced scorecard does not favor the financial per-spective; rather, it is linked to the budget process by (1) highlight-ing leading indicators; (2) balancing the financial, customer, internal process, and innovation and improvement perspectives; and (3) helping managers communicate strategic goals to all stakeholders.

Key Terms

Activity-based budgeting (ABB). A form of budgeting based on activity-based costing (ABC) that focuses on the cost of the activities involved in all functional areas of an organization.

Activity-based costing (ABC). A process by which managers identify the cost of resources, allocate these costs to activities, and then allocate the cost of activities to products.

Allocated costs. Non-production-related costs—such as rent, insurance, and administrative costs—that are allocated to individual units' operating budgets based on that unit's output.

Balanced scorecard. A method of translating an organization's strategic mission into multiple and linked objectives, focusing on financial, customer, internal business, and innovation and learning perspectives.

Budget. An organization's action plan, translating strategic objectives into measurable quantities that express the expected resources required and returns anticipated over a certain period of time.

Capital budget. A schedule detailing planned investment in capital assets, property, and equipment.

Capital budgeting. A method of evaluating investment proposals to determine whether they are financially sound, and to allocate limited capital resources to the most attractive proposals.

Cash budget. A plan or schedule for expected cash inflows and outflows.

Financial budget. The part of the master budget that includes the budgeted balance sheet, the capital budget, the cash budget, and the budgeted statement of cash flows. The financial budget describes the expected sources of capital required to support the operating budget.

Fixed budget. A budget in which the amounts are fixed over the budget period.

Fixed costs. Costs that remain the same through a wide range of production and sales volumes.

Flexible budget. A budget that can be "flexed" or adjusted when variances are computed to recognize the actual revenues and costs.

Gross margin. Gross profit divided by total revenue. Gross profit is total revenue minus cost of goods sold.

Incremental budgeting. A method of budgeting in which data from historical figures is used to establish a basis for future assumptions.

Kaizen budgeting. A form of budgeting that strives for continuous cost improvement or reduction.

Master budget. The umbrella budget that summarizes and integrates all the individual budgets within an organization.

Net present value. The current value of a future stream of cash flows, based on specific interest rate assumptions.

Operating budget. The part of the master budget that includes the expected revenues and costs summarized in the budgeted income statement.

Operating income. Revenue less cost of goods sold and selling, general, and administrative costs.

Participatory budgeting. A budgeting approach that incorporates input from line managers in formulating assumptions and goals.

Revenue per employee. A measure of productivity, calculated by dividing total revenues by the number of full-time employees.

Rolling budget. A plan that is continually being updated so that the budget time frame remains stable while the actual periods covered by the budget change. At the end of each period (month, quarter, or year), a future period is added to the budget.

Run rate. An estimate of a future cost or revenue amount based solely on the current cost or revenue level.

SG&A. Selling, general, and administrative costs.

Static budget. A budget that remains unchanged throughout the budget period based on one set of expected outputs. Variances are computed at the end of the budget period.

Top-down budgeting. A budgeting approach in which individual departmental goals are set by senior management.

Variable costs. Costs that fluctuate with incremental changes in output.

Variance. The difference between an actual amount and a budgeted amount in a financial budget plan.

Zero-based budgeting. The method of beginning each new budgeting process from a zero base, or from the ground up, as though the budget were being prepared for the first time. Every assumption and proposed expenditure receives a critical review.

To Learn More

Articles

Boesen, Thomas. "New Tools for a New Corporate Culture: The Budget-less Revolution." *Balanced Scorecard Report*, January 2002.

Borealis, Europe's leading polyolefin plastics manufacturer, replaced its traditional budget process with four core management systems, including the balanced scorecard. In a Q&A with the *Balanced Scorecard Report*, Thomas Boesen, the company's former financial controller, describes the new budgeting and planning approach. One by-product of the new program: four systems focused on the company's different needs eliminated much of the complexity, confusion, and inflexibility of the old budgeting system.

Gary, Loren. "Breaking the Budget Impasse." *Harvard Management Update*, May 2003.

Has your company's budget process helped you do a better job of belt-tightening during the current slowdown? Chances are that it hasn't. You hate the entire budget process, and you never see it pay off. So why do you keep doing it the same old way? Read what the experts have to say about not only changing your budgeting process, but whether your company should dispense with budgets entirely. The reality is that your budgeting process should be a tool for achieving strategic alignment, not for driving you insane.

Horvath, Peter, and Ralf Sauter. "Why Budgeting Fails: One Management System Is Not Enough." *Balanced Scorecard Report*, September 2004.

It's inefficient, ages too quickly, and is out of sync with the strategic plan. No wonder so many executives hate toiling over the annual budget. But, says Peter Horvath (Europe's leading authority on management accounting, controlling, and budgeting), don't look to the budget as the sole management system. Horvath and his associate Ralf Sauter describe six ways to fix budgeting, including integrating it with such systems as the balanced scorecard, so that it supports strategy execution in today's fast-changing environment.

Kaplan, Robert S., and David P. Norton. "The Balanced Scorecard: Measures That Drive Performance." *Harvard Business Review* On-Point Enhanced Edition, February 2000.

Kaplan and Norton developed a "balanced scorecard" performance measurement system that allows executives to view a company from several perspectives simultaneously. The scorecard includes financial measures that reveal the results of actions already taken, as well as three sets of operational measures that show customer satisfaction, internal processes, and the organization's ability to learn and improve. Creating a balanced scorecard requires translating a company's strategy and mission statement into specific goals and measures. Managers then track those measures as they work toward their goals.

Kaplan, Robert S., and David P. Norton. "Linking Strategy to Planning and Budgeting." *Balanced Scorecard Report*, May 2000.

Kaplan and Norton show how traditional budgeting practices can be made more responsive to a company's rapidly changing needs. They urge managers not just to focus on the operational budget, but to pay attention to the strategy budget as well, because that's what finances the initiatives that facilitate company growth. Managers also need to avoid falling into the trap of thinking that initiatives are ends in themselves. Rather, initiatives are the means by which a company accomplishes its strategic objectives.

Norton, David P., and Philip W. Peck. "Linking Operations to Strategy and Budgeting." *Balanced Scorecard Report*, September 2006.

In part 1 of this two-part series, Linking Strategy and Planning to Budgets, David P. Norton made the case for a new expense category, STRATEX, dedicated to funding strategic initiatives—the means by which the enterprise carries out strategy. In part 2, Norton and Philip W. Peck argue that successful strategy execution requires more than just a separate strategy budget: the organization must link both strategy and operations to the budget—and do so in a way that is transparent (thus easy to analyze and revise) and future focused. Causal models, driver-based planning, and adaptive tools such as rolling forecasts together constitute just such an integrating mechanism that can also give organizations more information (the whys, not just the whats), flexibility, and agility—vital capabilities in a competitive, fast-changing world.

Wardell, Charles. "High-Performance Budgeting." *Harvard Management Update*, January 1999.

No one looks forward to the budgeting process. It's most often viewed as an unproductive exercise that steals time from your real job. However, the budget can be a powerful instrument for helping with forecasting, planning, and employee involvement. To accomplish this, you must first reengineer the budgeting process. Then you have to rethink how you use the budget itself. The traditional budget and the budgeting process are not adequate for today's economy. Some key flaws are the inability to quantify significant metrics such as innovation and quality and the tendency to compartmentalize a company into small units, providing departments with no incentive to look at the big picture. *HMU* presents a new approach to budgeting by offering a six-point checklist that shows how to turn your budgeting process, and the resulting budget, into powerful tools.

Books

Harvard Business School Publishing. *Harvard Business Essentials Guide to Finance for Managers*. Boston: Harvard Business School Press, 2002.

Calculating and assessing the overall financial health of the business is an important part of any managerial position. From reading and deciphering financial statements, to understanding net present value, to calculating return on investment, *Finance for Managers* provides the fundamentals of financial literacy. Easy to use and nontechnical, this helpful guide gives managers the smart advice they need to increase their impact on financial planning, budgeting, and forecasting.

Hope, Jeremy, and Robin Fraser. *Beyond Budgeting: How Managers Can Break Free from the Annual Performance Trap*. Boston: Harvard Business School Press, 2004.

The traditional annual budgeting process—characterized by fixed targets and performance incentives—is time consuming, overcentralized, and outdated. Worse, it often causes dysfunctional and unethical managerial behavior. Based on an intensive, international study into pioneering companies, *Beyond Budgeting* offers an alternative, coherent management model that overcomes the limitations of traditional budgeting. Focused around achieving sustained improvement relative to competitors, it provides a guiding framework for managing in the twenty-first century.

Kaplan, Robert S., and David P. Norton. *The Strategy-Focused Organization: How Balanced Scorecard Companies Thrive in the New Business Environment*. Boston: Harvard Business School Press, 2000.

In this book, Kaplan and Norton describe how the concept of the balanced scorecard has progressed beyond its original usefulness as a tool to measure performance to a way of actually effecting strategic change. Using examples drawn from company experiences, the authors show how the balanced scorecard can help the strategy-focused organization achieve nonlinear performance breakthroughs.

Simons, Robert. *Performance Measurement and Control Systems for Implementing Strategy*. Upper Saddle River, NJ: Prentice Hall, 2000.

Simons presents a coherent body of practical theory that shows how new accounting and control tools can be used to implement strategy. He shows how techniques for performance measurement and control, aligning performance goals and incentives, and managing strategic risk can be implemented by managers to achieve profit goals and strategies.

•

Sources for Preparing a Budget

The following sources aided in development of this book:

Harvard Business School Publishing. "High-Performance Budgeting." *Harvard Management Update*, January 1999.

Harvard Business School Publishing. "Preparing a Budget." *Harvard ManageMentor* eLearning program, Personal Insight.

Horngren, Charles T., George Foster, and Srikant M. Datar. *Cost Accounting: A Managerial Emphasis*. Upper Saddle River, NJ: Prentice Hall, 1997.

Kaplan, Robert S., and Robin Cooper. *Cost and Effect: Using Integrated Cost Systems to Drive Profitability and Performance*. Boston: Harvard Business School Press, 1998.

Kaplan, Robert S., and David P. Norton. "The Balanced Scoreboard— Measures That Drive Performance." *Harvard Business Review*, January–February 1992.

Kaplan, Robert S., and David P. Norton. *The Strategy-Focused Organization: How Balanced Scorecard Companies Thrive in the New Business Environment*. Boston: Harvard Business School Press, 2001.

Marks, Eileen R., associate publisher, Harvard Business School Publishing. Personal conversation, fall 2000.

Narayanan, V. G., associate professor, Harvard Business School. Personal conversations, fall 2000.

Simons, Robert. *Performance Measurement and Control Systems for Implementing Strategy*. Upper Saddle River, NJ: Prentice Hall, 2000.

How to Order

Harvard Business Press publications are available worldwide from your local bookseller or online retailer.

You can also call:
1-800-668-6780

Our product consultants are available to help you 8:00 a.m.–6:00 p.m., Monday–Friday, Eastern Time. Outside the U.S. and Canada, call: 617-783-7450.

Please call about special discounts for quantities greater than ten.

You can order online at:
www.HBSPress.org